10 Questions

For Every Chapter of the Gospel of Matthew

MARI RODRIGUEZ

WESTBOW
PRESS®
A DIVISION OF THOMAS NELSON
& ZONDERVAN

WestBow Press books may be ordered through booksellers or by contacting:

WestBow Press
A Division of Thomas Nelson & Zondervan
1663 Liberty Drive
Bloomington, IN 47403
www.westbowpress.com
1 (866) 928-1240

ISBN: 978-1-5127-5323-3 (sc)
ISBN: 978-1-5127-5322-6 (e)

Library of Congress Control Number: 2016913388

Print information available on the last page.

WestBow Press rev. date: 08/11/2016

For Mom and Dad,
the ones who introduced me to Jesus.

Acknowledgments

I want to express my thanks to my youth leaders Dena and Hershey Gehris. You all planted the question and answer seed in my heart. I learned a lot playing Bible trivia! You felt like you didn't know what you were doing, but God had a plan. Thank you, Dena, for showing me what a strong Christian warrior lady looks like.

Thank you to my pastors Dale and Martha Rose, who taught me, corrected me, forced me out of my comfort zone, and raised a leader. Martha, you are the queen of "sink or swim." You trained me to be a swimmer. Pastor, you are a true servant of God's people, a roll-up-your-sleeves kind of leader—one I hope to be like.

Thanks to Matt and Heather Varnell, who taught me that leaders are the first ones to church (even if you live far), the ones who set up, the ones who intercede, the ones who minister, the ones who clean up, the ones who leave last, and the ones God rewards when no one is looking. Matt, you taught me the importance of prayer, and I am forever grateful.

To Shannon Rose, you are my biggest fan and supporter. Thank you for testing out my questions and for always believing in me. Thank you for your friendship and your love and for saying the hard things when I needed to hear them!

Thank you to Cendy and Annabell for asking for Bible study questions! Cendy, Annabell will want to race you through this book and gloat if she gets more right than you. You'd better study up!

Mary Martinez, thank you for teaching, listening, guiding, and instructing me and for the hug on my first day in a new place. The Lord knew I needed you next to me!

Thank you, family prayer group, for keeping my efforts in prayer every day. Daddy, Mom, and Conrad, praise the Lord! Here it is!

Introduction

Does this happen to you? You set out to read your Bible with great intentions and expectations and, as you read, your mind starts to wander. You're still reading, but at the end of the chapter, you realize that as your eyes scanned the page and read the words, your brain was thinking about other things. Now that you're finished, you can't really remember what you read.

Good news. You're not alone!

The purpose of *10 Questions* is to help you remember what you read by training you to observe details about what is happening in each chapter. As you search for the answers, you'll train yourself to notice where things are happening, who is there, who is speaking, and who is being spoken to.

Each answer to each question is found in the text, so there's no need to worry if you're not a Bible scholar! If you read, you'll find the answer! And you'll be impressed by how much information you remember!

10 Questions is also a great tool that helps motivate you to read since you're reading with a purpose. It helps make Bible reading approachable and fun!

How to Use *10 Questions*

1. Read the chapter.

2. Answer the questions by searching the text for answers.
   10 Questions is meant to be used in an "open book" fashion. Do not expect to remember all the answers from memory. Verse numbers are provided to help you pinpoint your search.

3. Write your answers.

4. Check your answers in the back of the book.

5. Move on to the next chapters.

Matthew 1

Read Matthew 1, then answer these ten questions:

1. Who begot Boaz? (v. 5)

2. Who begot Jehoshaphat? (v. 8)

3. Where were Jeconiah and his brothers carried away to? (v. 11)

4. How many generations are there from Abraham to David? (v. 17)

5. How many generations are there from the captivity in Babylon to Christ? (v. 17)

6. What happened to Mary after she was betrothed to Joseph, before they came together? (v. 18)

7. Who told Joseph not to be afraid to take Mary as his wife? (v. 20)

8. Why was He to be named Jesus? (v. 21)

9. What does the name *Immanuel* mean? (v. 23)

10. Did Joseph obey the angel? (v. 24)

Matthew 2

Read Matthew 2, then answer these ten questions:

1. What was the question the wise men asked? (v. 2)

2. Who was troubled when he heard the wise men's question? (v. 3)

3. Where was the Christ to be born? (v. 5)

4. How did they know where the Christ was to be born? (vv. 5, 6)

5. How did the wise men find the young child? (v. 9)

6. Who was the child with when the wise men came into the house? (v. 11)

7. What did the wise men do when they saw the young child? (v. 11)

8. Where did the angel instruct Joseph to go? (v. 13)

9. Herod ordered children to be put to death according to three things. They had to be male and what else? (v. 16)

10. How did Joseph know it was safe to return to Israel? (vv. 19, 20)

Matthew 3

Read Matthew 3, then answer these ten questions:

1. What was John the Baptist's main message? (v. 2)

2. Who was Isaiah the prophet talking about when he mentioned "the voice of one crying in the wilderness"? (vv. 1–3)

3. Where was John baptizing people? (v. 6)

4. What did John the Baptist call the Pharisees and Sadducees when they came to his baptism? (v. 7)

5. Why would a tree be cut down and thrown into the fire? (v. 10)

6. What will happen to the chaff? (v. 12)

7. What city did Jesus come from to be baptized? (v. 13)

8. Who said, "I need to be baptized by you"? (v. 14)

9. What opened when Jesus came out of the water? (v. 16)

10. Where did the voice in verse 17 come from? (v. 17)

Matthew 4

Read Matthew 4, then answer these ten questions:

1. Who was Jesus to be tempted by? (v. 1)

2. How many days had Jesus fasted for? (v. 2)

3. What did the devil show Jesus from the exceedingly high mountain? (v. 8)

4. Who ministered to Jesus when the devil left him? (v. 11)

5. After what event did Jesus depart to Galilee? (v. 12)

6. Who prophesied what is said in verses 15 and 16? (v. 14)

7. What sea were Peter and Andrew casting a net into? (v. 18)

8. Who was John's brother? (v. 21)

9. Name three things Jesus went about doing in Galilee. (v. 23)

10. Great multitudes followed Jesus from where? (v. 25)

Matthew 5

Read Matthew 5, then answer these ten questions:

1. Who does the kingdom of heaven belong to? (v. 3)

2. What is the promise for those who hunger and thirst for righteousness? (v. 6)

3. Who shall see God? (v. 8)

4. What shall the peacemakers be called? (v. 9)

5. Why should you be glad when people revile and persecute you? (v. 12)

6. What is the only good use for salt that has lost its flavor? (v. 13)

7. Who is in danger of the judgment? (v. 22)

8. What should you do to your right eye if it causes you to sin? (v. 29)

9. How many miles should you go with someone who compels you to go one mile? (v. 41)

10. Who is the "he" mentioned in verse 45? (v. 45)

Matthew 6

Read Matthew 6, then answer these ten questions:

1. What kind of people "sound a trumpet" when they do a good deed? (v. 2)

2. How do the heathens pray? (v. 7)

3. What happens if you do not forgive men their trespasses? (v. 15)

4. Who has a sad countenance while fasting? (v. 16)

5. Where should you *not* lay up for yourselves treasures? (v. 19)

6. What are the pitfalls of laying up your treasures on earth? (v. 19)

7. Who can serve two masters? (v. 24)

8. Who does not sow, reap, or gather into barns? (v. 26)

9. Who does not toil or spin? (v. 28)

10. What should be sought first? (v. 33)

Matthew 7

Read Matthew 7, then answer these ten questions:

1. What will happen if you judge? (v. 2)

2. What is in your own eye? (v. 3)

3. Where should you not cast your pearls? (v. 6)

4. What happens if you knock? (v. 7)

5. Where does the wide or broad gate lead to? (v. 13)

6. Which way is difficult? (v. 14)

7. How can you tell a wolf in sheep's clothing? (vv. 15, 16)

8. List three things that many will say to have done in the Lord's name. (v. 22)

9. Whoever hears Jesus's sayings and does them is likened to what? (v. 24)

10. What was different about the way Jesus taught as opposed to the scribes? (v. 29)

Matthew 8

Read Matthew 8, then answer these ten questions:

1. To whom did Jesus say, "I am willing; be cleansed"? (vv. 2, 3)

2. What was wrong with the centurion's servant? (v. 6)

3. What was Peter's mother-in-law ailing from? (v. 14)

4. What did Jesus cast out the spirits with? (v. 16)

5. Which prophet was quoted as saying, "He Himself took our infirmities and bore our sicknesses"? (v. 17)

6. What was Jesus doing when the great tempest arose and the boat was covered with waves? (v. 24)

7. How did Jesus calm the winds and sea? (v. 26)

8. Where was Jesus when he met two demon-possessed men? (v. 28)

9. Where were the two demon-possessed men coming out of? (v. 28)

10. What did the whole city beg Jesus to do? (v. 34)

Matthew 9

Read Matthew 9, then answer these ten questions:

1. What did Jesus say to the paralytic who upset the scribes? (v. 2)

2. Who was sitting at the tax office? (v. 9)

3. According to the Pharisees, who was Jesus eating with? (v. 11)

4. Who did Jesus say He came to call? (v. 13)

5. Who came to ask Jesus why His disciples didn't fast? (v. 14)

6. What was the woman with the flow of blood trying to touch? (v. 21)

7. Who was crying out and saying, "Son of David, have mercy on us!"? (v. 27)

8. What was Jesus's stern warning to the two healed blind men? (v. 30)

9. What happened when the demon was cast out of the mute, demon-possessed man? (v. 33)

10. Why was Jesus moved with compassion for the multitude? (v. 36)

Matthew 10

Read Matthew 10, then answer these ten questions:

1. What power did Jesus give to His twelve disciples? (v. 1)

2. Who is Andrew's brother? (v. 2)

3. What was Matthew's profession? (v. 3)

4. Who was a Canaanite? (v. 4)

5. Who did Jesus refer to as the "lost sheep"? (v. 6)

6. What should be done when you depart a place that will not receive your words? (v. 14)

7. What should be spoken in the light? (v. 27)

8. What did Jesus say He came to bring? (v. 34)

9. Who is not worthy of Jesus? (v. 37)

10. He who receives Jesus also receives whom? (v. 40)

Matthew 11

Read Matthew 11, then answer these ten questions:

1. Who did John send to ask Jesus if He was the Coming One? (vv. 2, 3)

2. What were the disciples to tell John? (v. 4)

3. Who is greater than John the Baptist? (v. 11)

4. Why did Jesus rebuke the cities in which most of his mighty works had been done? (v. 20)

5. Who was Jesus speaking to when he said, "For if the mighty works which were done in you had been done in Tyre and Sidon, they would have repented long ago"? (v. 21)

6. Who is the "you" that Jesus is speaking of when He says, "It will shall be more tolerable for the land of Sodom in the day of judgment than for you." (v. 23)

7. Who were "these things" revealed to? (v. 25)

8. Who were "these things" hidden from? (v. 25)

9. Who delivered all things to Jesus? (v. 27)

10. What will Jesus give to those who labor and are heavy laden? (v. 29)

Matthew 12

Read Matthew 12, then answer these ten questions:

1. Who entered the house of God and ate the showbread? (vv. 3, 4)

2. Who was the showbread for? (v. 4)

3. Who are the "they" that asked Jesus if it was lawful to heal on the Sabbath? (v. 10)

4. What did Jesus do for the man with the withered hand? (v. 13)

5. What did the Pharisees plot? (v. 14)

6. According to the Isaiah prophecy, the Gentiles would trust what? (v. 21)

7. What does an evil and adulterous generation seek? (v. 39)

8. Who repented at the preaching of Jonah? (v. 41)

9. What does an unclean spirit seek when it goes out of a man? (v. 43)

10. Who did Jesus say are His brother and sister and mother? (v. 50)

Matthew 13

Read Matthew 13, then answer these ten questions:

1. Where did Jesus preach from? (v. 2)

2. Where did the seed fall first? (v. 4)

3. Where did the seeds that were scorched by the sun land? (v. 5)

4. Who desired to see what the disciples were seeing? (v. 17)

5. What does the wicked one come and snatch away? (v. 19)

6. Who is represented by the seed sown among the thorns? (v. 22)

7. What was sown among the wheat? (v. 25)

8. How did Jesus speak to people who fulfilled prophecy? (vv. 34, 35)

9. Where was Jesus when people were offended at Him? (vv. 54–57)

10. Why did He not do many mighty works there? (v. 58)

Matthew 14

Read Matthew 14, then answer these ten questions:

1. For whose sake did Herod put John the Baptist in prison? (v. 3)

2. Who counted John the Baptist as a prophet? (v. 5)

3. What was Herodias's daughter's reward for dancing for Herod? (v. 8)

4. Why did the disciples want Jesus to send the multitudes away? (v. 15)

5. How many loaves did they have? (v. 17)

6. How many fish did they have? (v. 17)

7. How did Peter ask Jesus to prove that it was Him? (v. 28)

8. Why was Peter afraid? (v. 30)

9. What was the reaction of those who were in the boat? (v. 33)

10. Where did they land when they crossed over? (v. 34)

Matthew 15

Read Matthew 15, then answer these ten questions:

1. Where were the scribes and Pharisees from? (v. 1)

2. What did the disciples not do before they ate bread? (v. 2)

3. Who was Jesus talking to when He said, "Hypocrites!"? (v. 1, 7)

4. What did Jesus say about the heart of those who honor Him with their lips? (v. 8)

5. What did those who honor Jesus with their lips do in vain? (v. 9)

6. What defiles a man? (v. 11)

7. What happens when the blind lead the blind? (v. 14)

8. Where do evil thoughts, murders, adulteries, fornications, thefts, false witness, and blasphemies come from? (v. 19)

9. What was wrong with the woman's daughter? (v. 22)

10. How many people did the seven loaves and few little fish feed? (v. 38)

Matthew 16

Read Matthew 16, then answer these ten questions:

1. The Pharisees and Sadducees could discern the face of the sky, but not what? (v. 3)

2. What is the only sign that would be given? (v. 4)

3. What did the disciples think Jesus was referring to when He warned them in verse 6? (v. 6, 7)

4. What did "leaven of the Pharisees and Sadducees" really mean? (v. 12)

5. Who did men say that Jesus was? (v. 13, 14)

6. Who did Peter say that Jesus was? (v. 16)

7. Where would Jesus go to suffer many things? (v. 21)

8. Who said, "Far be it from You, Lord; this shall not happen to You!" (v. 22)

9. Jesus said if anyone desires to come after Him, what three things must he or she do? (v. 24)

10. How will each one be rewarded? (v. 27)

Matthew 17

Read Matthew 17, then answer these ten questions:

1. Who was lead up on a high mountain by themselves? (v. 1)

2. Who appeared to them? (v. 3)

3. What did Peter want to make for Jesus, Moses, and Elijah? (v. 4)

4. When was it okay for Peter, James, and John to tell about the vision? (v. 9)

5. Who tried but could not cure the epileptic boy? (v. 16)

6. Why could the disciples not cast out the demon? (v. 20)

7. What two things were also needed to cast out that kind of demon? (v. 21)

8. Where were they staying when Jesus said he'd be betrayed in the hands of men? (v. 22)

9. What kind of tax were they to pay in Capernaum? (v. 24)

10. What was Peter to do with the money from the fish's mouth? (v. 27)

Matthew 18

Read Matthew 18, then answer these ten questions:

1. What question did the disciples ask? (v. 1)

2. Whoever does what as the little child is the greatest in the kingdom of heaven? (v. 4)

3. What should you do if your hand or foot causes you to sin? (v. 8)

4. What is better than having two eyes and being cast into hell fire? (v. 9)

5. What did the Son of Man come to save? (v. 11)

6. What should you do if your brother sins against you? (v. 15)

7. If he hears you, then what have you gained? (v. 15)

8. What will be loosed in heaven? (v. 18)

9. What will happen if two of you agree on earth concerning anything you ask? (v. 19)

10. How many times should you forgive? (v. 22)

Matthew 19

Read Matthew 19, then answer these ten questions:

1. What question did the Pharisees ask? (v. 3)

2. What shall the two become? (v. 5)

3. What should man not separate? (v. 6)

4. Why did Moses allow a certificate of divorce? (v. 8)

5. What saying was Jesus talking about when He said, "All cannot accept this saying …"? (v. 10, 11)

6. Who did Jesus tell His disciples to allow to come to Him? (v. 14)

7. Who is the only One that is good? (v. 17)

8. What did Jesus say had to be done in order to enter into life? (v. 17)

9. What three things did the rich, young ruler have to do in order to be perfect? (v. 21)

10. Why did the rich, young ruler go away sorrowful? (v. 22)

Matthew 20

Read Matthew 20, then answer these ten questions:

1. What was the wage for the laborers per day? (v. 2)

2. In what hour were the last laborers hired? (v. 6, 7)

3. Why did the first laborers expect to receive more pay? (v. 10, 12)

4. What did Jesus say to the disciples on the side of the road on the way to Jerusalem? (v. 17, 18, 19)

5. What did the mother of Zebedee's sons ask for? (v. 21)

6. Who was "greatly displeased" with the two brothers? (v. 24)

7. What city were they leaving when they encountered the two blind men? (v. 29)

8. Who warned the blind men to be quiet? (v. 31)

9. What question did Jesus ask the two blind men? (v. 32)

10. What did the blind men do after receiving their sight? (v. 34)

Matthew 21

Read Matthew 21, then answer these ten questions:

1. What kind of animal would the two disciples find tied up? (v. 2)

2. Who did Jesus drive out of the temple? (v. 12)

3. Where did Jesus lodge after leaving Jerusalem? (v. 17)

4. What kind of tree had nothing but leaves on it? (v. 19)

5. What ultimately happened to the fig tree? (v. 19)

6. What was the father's request to his two sons? (v. 28)

7. What was the first son's response to his father's request? (v. 29)

8. Who beat, killed, and stoned the landowner's servants? (v. 33–35)

9. Why did the landowner send his son? (v. 37)

10. Which stone was Jesus talking about when he said, "Whoever falls on this stone will be broken …"? (v. 42–44)

Matthew 22

Read Matthew 22, then answer these ten questions:

1. What is like a certain king who arranged a marriage for his son? (v. 2)

2. Who was not worthy to attend the wedding? (v. 8)

3. Who went out into the highways to find people to attend the wedding? (v. 8, 9)

4. What happened to the man without the wedding garment? (v. 12, 13)

5. Who did the Pharisees send to ask Jesus about paying taxes? (v. 15, 16)

6. What should be rendered to Caesar? (v. 21)

7. How many brothers did the woman marry in the Sadducees' scenario? (v. 26)

8. What was the occupation of the man who asked Jesus, "Teacher, which is the great commandment in the law?" (v. 35)

9. On which two commandments hand all the law and the prophets? (v. 37–40)

10. The Pharisees said that the Christ was the Son of whom? (v. 41, 42)

Matthew 23

Read Matthew 23, then answer these ten questions:

1. Jesus told the multitudes to observe what the Pharisees say to observe but not to do what? (v. 3)

2. Why did Jesus tell the multitudes not to do according to the works of the Pharisees? (v. 3)

3. He who is greatest among you shall be what? (v. 11)

4. What did the blind guides say to swear by? (v. 16)

5. Who swears by the throne of God and by Him who sits on it? (v. 22)

6. What were the weightier matters of the law neglected by the Pharisees? (v. 23)

7. What would happen if the Pharisee would clean the inside of the cup and dish? (v. 26)

8. What made the scribes and Pharisees like whitewashed tombs? (v. 27)

9. What will the scribes and Pharisees do with the prophets, wise men, and scribes that Jesus will send? (v. 34)

10. Who was Jesus talking about when he said "the one who kills the prophets and stones those who are sent to her" (v. 37)

Matthew 24

Read Matthew 24, then answer these ten questions:

1. Who will the many that come claim to be? (v. 5)

2. Wars, rumors of wars, famines, and pestilences are all the beginning of what? (v. 6, 8)

3. What will happen to the love of many? (v. 12)

4. What will happen after the gospel of the kingdom is preached in all the world? (v. 14)

5. Where will those who are in Judea flee to when the "abomination of desolation" stands in the holy place? (v. 15, 16)

6. What will happen to the days for the elect's sake? (v. 22)

7. What is near when the branches of the fig tree become tender and put forth leaves? (v. 32)

8. Who, besides the Father, knows the day or the hour of the coming of the Son of Man? (v. 36)

9. When two women will be grinding at the mill, what happens next? (v. 41)

10. What will become of the faithful and wise servant when the master returns? (v. 46, 47)

Matthew 25

Read Matthew 25, then answer these ten questions:

1. How many of the virgins were wise? (v. 2)

2. What made five of the virgins foolish? (v. 2)

3. Where did the door that was shut lead to? (v. 10)

4. What did the servant who was given one talent do with it? (v. 18)

5. Where will the unprofitable servant be cast? (v. 30)

6. When will the Son of Man sit on the throne of His glory? (v. 31)

7. What will He do with all the nations that will be gathered before Him? (v. 32)

8. To the people, on which hand will He say, "Depart from Me ..."? (v. 41)

9. Who are "these" when Jesus says, "And these will go away into everlasting punishment ..."? (v. 41, 46)

10. Where will the righteous go? (v. 46)

Matthew 26

Read Matthew 26, then answer these ten questions:

1. What will happen after the Passover? (v. 2)

2. Who assembled at the palace of Caiaphas, the high priest? (v. 3)

3. What city was Simon the leper's house in? (v. 6)

4. Where did the woman pour the costly, fragrant oil? (v. 7)

5. How much was Judas Iscariot paid to deliver Jesus to the chief priests? (v. 15)

6. How did the disciples know that one of them would betray Jesus? (v. 21)

7. What did they do before they went out to the Mount of Olives? (v. 30)

8. What did all the disciples do after Jesus was arrested? (v. 56)

9. What was Jesus responding to when He said, "It is as you said …"? (v. 63, 64)

10. How many times did Peter deny knowing Jesus? (v. 70, 72, 74, 75)

Matthew 27

Read Matthew 27, then answer these ten questions:

1. What was the name of the governor? (v. 2)

2. What was bought with the thirty pieces of silver? (v. 7)

3. Who said, "Have nothing to do with that just Man, for I have suffered many things today in a dream because of Him"? (v. 17–19)

4. How did those who passed by ask Jesus to prove that He was the Son of God? (v. 39, 40)

5. During which hours was there darkness over all the land? (v. 45)

6. Who did some of those who stood there think He was calling for? (v. 47)

7. What was torn in two at the time of Jesus's death? (v. 51)

8. What three things do we know about Joseph by reading verse 57? (v. 57)

9. Who was sitting opposite the tomb? (v. 61)

10. Who did the chief priests and Pharisees fear would steal Jesus's body? (v. 64)

Matthew 28

Read Matthew 28, then answer these ten questions:

1. Who rolled back the stone from the door? (v. 2)

2. The angel's countenance was like what? (v. 3)

3. What was the guards' reaction to the angel? (v. 4)

4. Where did the angel say that Jesus was going? (v. 7)

5. Who met the women as they went to tell the disciples? (v. 9)

6. What was Jesus's word to the women as they met him? (v. 9)

7. Why did the elders and chief priests pay the soldiers a large sum of money? (v. 12, 13)

8. How many disciples went away into Galilee? (v. 16)

9. Who had all authority been given to? (v. 18)

10. What three things were the disciples instructed to go and do? (v. 19, 20)

Answers

Chapter 1

1. Salmon.

2. Asa.

3. Babylon.

4. Fourteen.

5. Fourteen.

6. She was found with child.

7. An angel of the Lord.

8. He will save all His people from their sins.

9. God with us.

10. Yes.

Chapter 2

1. Where is the King of the Jews?

2. Herod.

3. In Bethlehem.

4. It was written by the prophet.

5. The star went before them and stood over where the young Child was.

6. Mary, His mother.

7. They fell down and worshipped Him.

8. To Egypt.

9. Were in Bethlehem and all its districts; were two years old and under.

10. An angel appeared to him in a dream.

Chapter 3

1. "Repent, for the kingdom of heaven is at hand!"

2. John the Baptist.

3. In the Jordan (River).

4. A brood of vipers.

5. If it does not bear good fruit.

6. It will be burned up.

7. Galilee.

8. John (the Baptist).

9. The heavens.

10. Heaven.

Chapter 4

1. The devil.

2. Forty.

3. All the kingdoms of the world and their glory.

4. Angels.

5. The imprisonment of John the Baptist.

6. Isaiah.

7. The Sea of Galilee.

8. James.

9. Teaching, preaching, and healing.

10. Galilee, Decapolis, Jerusalem, Judea, and beyond the Jordan.

Chapter 5

1. The poor in spirit.
2. They shall be filled.
3. The pure in heart.
4. Sons of God.
5. For great is your reward in heaven.
6. To be thrown out and trampled underfoot by men.
7. Whoever is angry with his brother without a cause.
8. Pluck it out and cast it from you.
9. Two miles.
10. Your Father in heaven [God].

Chapter 6

1. Hypocrites.
2. In vain repetitions.
3. Neither will our Father forgive your trespasses.
4. Hypocrites.
5. On earth.
6. Moth and rust destroy; thieves break in and steal.
7. No one.
8. The birds of the air.
9. The lilies of the field.
10. The kingdom of God and His righteousness.

Chapter 7

1. You will be judged.
2. A plank.

3. Before swine.

4. It will be opened to you.

5. Destruction.

6. The way which leads to life; the narrow gate.

7. By their fruits.

8. Prophesied, cast out demons, done many wonders.

9. A wise man who built his house on the rock.

10. He taught them as one having authority.

Chapter 8

1. A leper.

2. He was paralyzed and dreadfully tormented.

3. Fever.

4. A word.

5. Isaiah.

6. Sleeping.

7. He rebuked them.

8. The country of the Gergesenes.

9. The tombs.

10. Depart from their region.

Chapter 9

1. "Your sins are forgiven you."

2. Matthew.

3. Tax collectors and sinners.

4. Sinners.

5. The disciples of John.

6. Jesus's garment.

7. Two blind men.

8. "See that no one knows it." (Don't tell anyone.)

9. The mute spoke.

10. They were weary and scattered like sheep having no shepherd.

Chapter 10

1. Power to cast out unclean spirits and to heal all kinds of sickness and disease.

2. Peter.

3. Tax collector.

4. Simon.

5. Israel.

6. Shake off the dust from your feet.

7. Whatever was told in the dark.

8. A sword.

9. He who loves father or mother, a son or daughter more than Him.

10. Him who sent (Jesus) Me.

Chapter 11

1. Two of his disciples.

2. The things they heard and saw.

3. He who is least in the kingdom of heaven.

4. Because they did not repent.

5. Chorazin and Bethsaida.

6. Capernaum.

7. Babes.

8. The wise and prudent.

9. His Father.

10. Rest.

Chapter 12

1. David and those who were with him.
2. The priests.
3. The Pharisees.
4. Healed him (restored the hand as whole as the other).
5. How they might destroy Him.
6. In His name.
7. A sign.
8. The men of Nineveh.
9. Rest.
10. Whoever does the will of His Father in heaven.

Chapter 13

1. A boat.
2. By the wayside.
3. On stony places.
4. Prophets and righteous men.
5. The word of the kingdom sown in people's hearts.
6. He who hears the word and the cares of this world and the deceitfulness of riches choke the word.
7. Tares.
8. He spoke to them in parables.
9. In His own country.
10. Because of their unbelief.

Chapter 14

1. Herodias.
2. The multitude.

3. John the Baptist's head on a platter.

4. So they could go buy food.

5. Five.

6. Two.

7. He told Jesus to command him to come to Him on the water.

8. He saw that the wind was boisterous.

9. They worshiped Him, saying, "Truly You are the Son of God."

10. The land of Gennesaret.

Chapter 15

1. Jerusalem.

2. Wash their hands.

3. The scribes and the Pharisees.

4. Their heart is far from Me.

5. Worship Him.

6. What comes out of the mouth.

7. They both fall into a ditch.

8. The heart.

9. She was demon possessed.

10. Four thousand besides women and children.

Chapter 16

1. The signs of the times.

2. The sign of the prophet Jonah.

3. The fact that they had taken no bread.

4. The doctrine of the Pharisees and Sadducees.

5. John the Baptist, Elijah, Jeremiah, or one of the prophets.

6. The Christ, the Son of the living God.

7. Jerusalem.

8. Peter.

9. Deny himself, take up his cross, and follow Me.

10. According to his works.

Chapter 17

1. Peter, James, and John.

2. Moses and Elijah.

3. Tabernacles.

4. After the Son of Man had risen from the dead.

5. The disciples.

6. Because of their unbelief.

7. Prayer and fasting.

8. In Galilee.

9. The temple tax.

10. Pay the temple tax.

Chapter 18

1. "Who then is greatest in the kingdom of heaven?"

2. Humbles himself.

3. Cut it off and cast it from you.

4. To enter into life with one eye.

5. That which was lost.

6. Go and tell him his fault.

7. Your brother.

8. Whatever you loose on earth.

9. It will be done for them.

10. Seventy times seven.

Chapter 19

1. "Is it lawful for a man to divorce his wife for just any reason?"

2. One flesh.

3. What God has joined together.

4. Because of the hardness of their hearts.

5. "It is better not to marry."

6. The little children.

7. God.

8. Keep the commandments.

9. Sell what he had, give to the poor, and follow Jesus.

10. Because he had great possessions.

Chapter 20

1. A denarius.

2. The eleventh hour.

3. They had worked all day.

4. He would be betrayed, condemned to death, crucified, and risen on the third day.

5. If her two sons can sit on the right and left of Jesus in His kingdom.

6. The ten; the rest of the disciples.

7. Jericho.

8. The multitude.

9. "What do you want me to do for you?"

10. They followed Jesus.

Chapter 21

1. A donkey.

2. Those who bought and sold in the temple, the money changers.

3. Bethany.

4. A fig tree.

5. It withered away.

6. "Son, go work today in my vineyard."

7. "I will not."

8. The vinedressers.

9. He thought they would respect his son.

10. The stone the builders rejected; the chief cornerstone.

Chapter 22

1. The kingdom of heaven.

2. Those who were invited.

3. Servants.

4. He was cast into outer darkness.

5. Their disciples with the Herodians.

6. The things that are Caesar's.

7. Seven.

8. A lawyer.

9. 1. You shall love the Lord your God with all your heart, with all your soul, and with all your mind 2. You shall love your neighbor as yourself.

10. David.

Chapter 23

1. Do not do according to their works.

2. Because they say and do not do.

3. Your servant.

4. The gold of the temple.

5. He who swears by heaven.

6. Justice, mercy, and faith.

7. The outside would be clean also.

8. They appear beautiful outwardly but inside are full of dead men's bones and all uncleanness.

9. Crucify, scourge, and persecute them.

10. Jerusalem.

Chapter 24

1. The Christ.

2. Sorrows.

3. It will grow cold.

4. The end will come.

5. To the mountains.

6. They will be shortened.

7. Summer.

8. No one.

9. One will be taken and the other left.

10. He will be made ruler of all the master's goods.

Chapter 25

1. Five.

2. They took their lamps and took no oil with them.

3. The wedding.

4. Dug in the ground and hid it.

5. Into the outer darkness.

6. When He comes in His glory.

7. Separate them.

8. Those on the left hand.

9. Those on the left hand.

10. Into eternal life.

Chapter 26

1. The Son of Man will be delivered up to be crucified.
2. The chief priests, the scribes, and the elders of the people.
3. Bethany.
4. On His head.
5. Thirty pieces of silver.
6. He told them.
7. Sung a hymn.
8. Forsook Him and fled.
9. The high priest saying, "Tell us if You are the Christ, the Son of God!"
10. Three.

Chapter 27

1. Pontius Pilate.
2. The potter's field.
3. Pilate's wife.
4. Come down from the cross.
5. From the sixth hour until the ninth hour.
6. Elijah.
7. The veil of the temple.
8. He was rich. He was from Arimathea. He had become a disciple of Jesus.
9. Mary Magdalene and the other Mary.
10. The disciples.

Chapter 28

1. An angel of the Lord.
2. Lightning.

3. They shook for fear of him and became like dead men.

4. To Galilee.

5. Jesus.

6. "Rejoice!"

7. To say that Jesus's disciples came at night and stole Him away while they slept.

8. Eleven.

9. Jesus.

10. Make disciples of all the nations, baptize them in the name of the Father, Son, and Holy Spirit, and teach them to observe all the things that He commanded.

After *10 Questions*

Now that you have practiced observation, move on to the next steps in good Bible study.

- **Interpretation.** What does the scripture mean to you? What does it say to you? Interpretation is the *meaning* of the scripture.

- **Application**. How will I take this scripture and apply it to my life? Do I need to make changes? What will I do in light of this scripture?

Let's try it. John 6:35 says, "And <u>Jesus</u> said to <u>them</u>, 'I am the **bread of life**. He who comes to Me shall never hunger, and he who believes in Me shall never thirst.'"

Observation asks, "Who is speaking? Who is 'them' that are being spoken to? Where are they? What did Jesus say about people who believe in Him?"

Interpretation thinks, *When Jesus says He's the Bread of Life, does He mean He's a loaf of bread? No! He means that if people will have Him in their lives, He'll keep them satisfied and happy!*

Application reflects. "If Jesus is the bread of life, do I have Him in *my* life? Have I let Him make *me* satisfied and happy? What can I do to make this happen?

Reading scripture is great. But every person who wants to become more familiar with God's word has to go beyond just reading—there's studying involved! *10 Questions* is the first step in a deeper understanding of scripture.

Printed in the United States
By Bookmasters